# ACAPULCO

TEXT: **J. GRAU**

1st. Edition, July 1978
I.S.B.N.
84-7424-014-X

GEOCOLOR® S.A.

This book is an interesting publication on one of the states of the Republic - Guerrero, deeply rooted in the history of our country as part of one of the viceregal provinces, being created a new state of the Republic of Mexico by decree on October 27th 1847 and bearing the name of the rebel general Vicente Guerrero.

The fundamental aim of this edition is to reproduce this region and show its vast possibilities for tourism.

The centre of world attraction is Acapulco, situated on the shores of the Pacific with the legend of the South Seas, which during the viceregal period was a focal point of trade between this continent and Asia. Once the navegational route was established, prosperous trading was built up and the merchandise was transported by the fantastic ships, La Nao from China and the Galeon from the Philippines. This exchange even influenced the European markets bringing silk, ivory and spices etc. In its turn New Spain paid for these products together with government expenses in the Philippines with silver coins whose "peso" was much appreciated in Asia.

A visit to Acapulco is the dream of many and there is good reason for this; its climate and waters can be enjoyed fully all the year round; a resort atmosphere has been created, having international attractions and all sorts of entertainment for the tourist.

We have discovered Zihuatanejo-Iztapa, two hundred kilometres to the Northeast of Acapulco, whose tourist development is already a positive attraction and is now in communication by air and road; there is a lot of fishing on these Pacific coasts and the food, especially the famous ceviche is a pleasure for all, and in addition there is the delicious tropical fruit.

In Acapulco it is still possible to find remains of the viceregal period such as the Fort of San Diego.

Acapulco has justly earned its fame: everything there invites one to enjoyment and the people are of the most hospitable; there are magnificent hotels of maximum confort, fine residences, hotel and tourist services at international standard; golf courses and tennis courts, all within everyone's reach. Mention must be made of its Convention Centre with its fine rooms and theatres with a seating capacity for up to 8,000 delegates.

Acapulco is well communicated nationally and internationally, having a splendid airport; also large numbers of visitors arrive by sea and by road.

A few kilometres from the city of Acapulco is Taxco, a relic of the viceregal period, the silver capital, famous for its craft work, where the tourist can find many places where he can acquire the loveliest silver ornaments, many of them real filigree, — along with other articles — all noteworthy products of the manual ability of the villages around Taxco.

An authentic jewel of Mexican baroque art is the XVIII century parish church of Santa Prisca described as one of the most outstanding of its kind; writers have said the "its artifices know how to combine salomonic columns, pilasters in the form of reversed pyramids, and rococo decoration in such a way that baroque style and its different variations is portrayed and synthesized in this admirable work of art".

The mine owner don Jose de la Borda was responsible for its construction after he had discovered one of the richest silver mines of the age.

An important feature of Guerrero, as we have already mentioned, is its handwork. Apart from the things made in Taxco, no less important are laquers from Olinala, pottery and ceramics from Xalitla, palm hats from Tlapa, San Luis Acatlan and Tlapehuala. There is also pottery from San Miguel Huapa and Toliman, embroidered skirts from Amatlan, masks from Tixlla and Chilapa, decorated bread and serviettes from Ixcateopan, machetes from Ayutla and Tecpan, leather goods from Pungarabato and Tlalchapa.

A visit to these towns in Guerrero must be top priority on the itinerary of any tourist coming to Mexico.

Lic. Miguel Alemán
Presidente del Consejo Nacional de Turismo
de la República Mexicana

*JUXTLAHUACA. Olmec cave painting representing a warrior (State of Guerrero).*

Guerrero State is an attractive geographical location comprising the Balsas basin and the rugged mountains of the Sierra Madre del Sur.
To the north, in the basin of the river Balsas, Guerrero State spills over onto a large plain, uninterrupted except for the occasional low hill. This is part of the great tropical Mexico, the rural Mexico of evergreen oaks, palo blanco and strawberry trees. It is also the historical Mexico, — the country watered not only by the generous valley of the river Balsas, the site of so many battles, but also by the blood of thousands of natives, — which now flowers in the achievement of its fruitful independence. To the south of the state, closing off the gradual opening out of the Balsas basin, is the rugged Sierra Madre del Sur. At an almost constant altitude of 2,000 metres, it is a great wall beyond which stretches the coastal Mexico of Guerrero State with its wide beaches and fine sand for the tourists who discover the sensual, the comfortable

aspect of Mexico, the captivating Mexico of Coyuca de Benitez, Zihuatanejo, and of course Acapulco.

## ACAPULCO

The known history of Acapulco (the name means "conquered place" according to some historians and "destroyed place" according to others) began towards the end of the XV century when a warlike campaign during the reign of Ahuitzotl succeeded in incorporating the city into the Aztec empire.
Some years later, the Spanish conquistadores made a port at Acapulco, and it was from there that Hurtado de Mendoza led an attack by sea against the coasts of New Spain in 1532.
Once the Philippines were occupied, Acapulco became the port of call for the Galleon from Manila and the Nao from China which arrived every year laden with priceless oriental merchandise from the capital of the Philippines. And it was the corsairs

CHILPANCINGO.

*Government Palace
(Mural paintings).*

and pirates who caused the gradual eclipse of the port of Acapulco in the XVII centlry. In this century Dutch and English pirates were so powerful in the waters of the Pacific that they even entered the bay of Acapulco, and being ambushed there, took possession of the galleons coming from the Philippines. This caused the Spaniards to open up a new route in the XVIII century for the transportation of merchandise from the Philippines. But Acapulco, in modern times, after experiencing Mexico's bitter struggle for independence, was able to acquire trade in a new type of merchandise equally valuable to that which used to arrive from the Orient. Today Acapulco is a haven for thousands upon thousands of tourists, for a jet society ready to leave its metal gold in exchange for the pleasurable gold of the unending sun of Acapulco, for the sea, the nights at Acapulco, this something, this everything that very few cities can offer. For

very few cities possess the natural charm of Acapulco, and very few have been able to complement their natural attractions and eternal summer time with the added delights of comfort and luxury, entertainment and pleasure created by the hand of man.
In one of the loveliest natural backgrounds in the world, amid luxuriant tropical vegetation and a splendid rocky coastline, Acapulco offers the widest possible range of pleasures ever dreamed of, from the simplest to the most sophisticated. Acapulco: the mere sight of the city is a pleasure in itself.
All the pleasures imaginable can become a reality here, and the most pleasurable of its realities is its beaches. These are all wonderful stretches of sand divided into two large groups. On the one side, those beginning in the west of the bay behind La Quebrada, stretching towards the port; and on the other, those that join with the Miguel Aleman coast,

Aprehensión de Cuauhtémoc ante Cortés (13 de agosto de 1521), al fondo, derrumbamiento de la cultura. Mexica, con el símbolo de la conquista de... en el esplendor de Tenochtitlan, Palacios de Moctezuma y rebelión

*TIXTLA. Monument to Vicente Guerrero.*

— a route that runs like a shuttle between these vast beaches with their fine sand, going from the port and along the back of the bay and ending at the promontory at the other end of the bay, the eastern point.

The first group of beaches is made up of a number of fascinating coves flanked by coconut trees and ending in steep cliffs. These are attractive beaches with a primaeval beauty whose vegetation reaches the nearby gardens with their tropical plants. They are beaches that are full of life, and hundreds of hotels give them a constant supply of tourists. Here life consists of sunny days and entertaining nights on the beaches of Angosta, el Patal, Caletilla, Caleta, Larga, Honda and Manzanillo: there is also the Roqueta beach on an island reached by motor boat from the Caleta beach. This is an unforgettable experience for any tourist. The motor boat with its glass bottom allows one to enjoy the unforgettable sight of the underwater scenery and the submerged statue of the Virgin of Guadalupe.

The second group of beaches along the Miguel Aleman coastline are vast and have less hotels, and these become gradually more luxurious as they leave the city area, some of them having their own beaches and parks. This tourist area has sumptuous night clubs, luxurious restaurants with a sophisticated cuisine, all types of exotic pleasures for the tourist including the Cultural Centre of Conventions close by the Icacos beach, which, together with the large beaches of Hornos and Condesa, makes up this attractive bathing area. Outside the bay of Acapulco, along the eastern side, some 22 kilometres from the city is what could be termed the third beach area of Acapulco. This is a hotel area of great luxury with buildings dotting the land around the vast, and seemingly infinite Revolcadero beach, a beach with fine sand and coconut trees opening out onto the sea where the most daring of water sports are practised.

But Acapulco is, as we have already said, something more than a series of wonderful beaches; it has succeeded in increasing its natural beauty and has made it more accessible with a network of sumptuous hotels. The Hotel Las Brisas situated on the headland at the eastern end of the bay offers its guests, besides its own beach, 200 swimming pools and a jeep per room. On the Revolcadero beach, the luxurious Acapulco Country Club and Acapulco Princess Hotels possessing every possible amenity, are both situated close to the sea shore and have a tropical cuisine with the most exquisite of dishes. The Miguel Aleman coastal area has two

luxurious hotels, — the Hyatt Regency and El Presidente, the latter famous for its revolutionary architecture. Actually, these beaches at Acapulco would not be as privileged as they are in spite of their excepcional beauty if it were not for the fringe of fine hotels, all of them with the height of comfort and many of them outstandingly luxurious, along the sea shore. These hotels, besides their enviable location and magnificent service, have a first class cuisine and include hundreds of typical restaurants, some of them right on the sea shore.

In fact the essence of Acapulco is the sea and its beaches and in spite of its history it has only one historical monument worthy of the name, — the San Diego Fort, a pentagonal fortress dating from the XVII century. It is true that in Acapulco there are no more monuments than those of its recently erected buildings and among these, together with the hotels, is the Cultural Centre and Centre for Conventions, a complex of unequalled beauty, in the middle of lovely gardens near to a golf course, with

*ALTAMIRANO - LAZARO CARDENAS (Monumental work by F. CANESSI).*

*ACAPULCO.*

conference halls equipped with the most modern simultaneous translation installations and closed circuit television; there are also exhibition rooms and even a theatre.

Acapulco has only existed in its present state for some 40 years and while it has not forgotten its most ancient history, it is creating a new type of history, made up of entertainment and pleasure, which is revealed in the best the city has to offer in this respect. The monuments at Acapulco are its beaches and the sea, where everyone can practise sea sports ranging from water skiing to fishing. The International Fishing Tournament is celebrated in Acapulco in the month of March.

The sea at Acapulco is a whirl of constant and varied entertainment. You can, for example, sail along the bay in the sunlight for two and a half hours on board the yacht Mexico-Fiesta, together with an orchestra and you will see the many panoramic views and all the charm of the city. If you are of a romantic turn of mind, or if a meeting in Acapulco gives you back that yearning for a return to the days of your youth, don't miss the same trip on the yacht Bonanza, — it's one long party with dancing in the moonlight, in the Acapulco moonlight, which has been said to be "the same moonlight that lit up Paradise when the first man and woman succumbed to its charm and discovered the meaning of love." The sea at Acapulco is well filled with fish; so much so in fact that on the quayside it is not difficult to find young boys throwing in their lines with three hooks on the end without any bait. After casting

*ACAPULCO. La Quebrada seen from the Hotel Mirador.*

*ACAPULCO. View from the sea.*

ACAPULCO. La Quebrada.

their lines they slowly draw them in and, as if by magic, there appears a fish on the end, sometimes caught by the mouth, sometimes by the belly and even by the tail. Fishing in Acapulco, not necessarily on the high seas where there are martin and swordfish etc., is a sport with a high rate of success. Success is even more assured if you like diving and go in for underwater fishing. If you do this, you will not only catch fish but also be able to see some fine underwater scenery and maybe the remains of a shipwreck. But possibly you will prefer the challenge of skiing with a parachute, surfing, or the excitement of the unique spectacle of "los clavistas" (high divers).

Every night from 9.30 and every hour until after midnight, Acapulco offers the most exciting of rites,

a rite which has already cost many lives, especially among the tourists, — the alarming spectacle of the high divers. On La Quebrada, at a height of 35 metres, lit up by arc lights, in an atmosphere of tense silence, the diver walks along a rocky cliff at the edge of the sea with the waves lashing down below. The diver calmly looks upwards to Heaven and makes a slow genuflexion in homage and as a prayer, for the diver both salutes the Virgin and begs for her protection. Ready now, saluting death like an ancient gladiator, the diver makes a perfect flying angel dive towards a specific point in the sea, towards a narrow, not very deep hollow, calculating at the same time the moment when the waves wash over the place so as not to be dashed against the sharp rocks of the cliff. But the danger of an almost

ACAPULCO.
*High diver
(clavadista)
at La
Quebrada.*

inevitable death does not paralyse the diver who flings himself into the sea in a slow fall that has all the beauty of flight. And the diver comes up unhurt from the waves. The tension breaks and there are shouts of applause and enthusiasm. The Virgin has worked a miracle. Although occasionally, and fortunately rarely, the miracle does not work and the diver, almost always an excessively daring tourist, dies on La Quebrada or emerges permanently damaged physically. In Acapulco sports and entertainment does not end in the sea. There is also hunting here. Nearby is the lagoon of Coyuca where caimans take the sun while in the undergrowth around are wild duck, deer, pumas, jaguars and tapirs... There are of course, less risky sports and also golf, tennis, riding, and may others similar to those you can practise at home.

However, Acapulco offers entertainment that is impossible to find at home, except if you happen to be Spanish and are used to bull fighting and jai

*ACAPULCO. La Quebrada (night view).*

alai, two of the many varied forms of entertainment Acapulco can offer you.

Every Sunday there is a bull-fight in the bull-ring at Acapulco. This is the Spanish festivity that stains the arena and the suit of the bull-fighter with blood. Now it is as much a Mexican as a Spanish celebration and often succeeds in generating real excitement among the spectators, This is essentially a brave spectacle of man facing beast in a sort of ballet in which death is a permanent presence.

Jai alai is the Basque pelota game, although there exists in Mexico a precedent of the jai alai which has given it its own peculiar characteristics and traditions; this is known as the Hachtli, a pelota game whose symbolism was used by the Aztecs to make performances in which the participants pretended to be supernatural beings who played with the sun or the moon in the sky.

The game of jai alai of which the inhabitants of Acapulco are so fond will not only entertain you

*ACAPULCO. Playa Langosta (also called Angusta).*

*Playa Roqueta. Donkey being fond of beer.*

*Beach on the Isle of La Roqueta.*

*Conch and coral seller at Playa de la Roqueta.*

Diver feeding fish with meat of echini which he has just caught.

The Virgin of Guadalupe. Bronze statue situated on the bottom of the sea in front of the Isle of la Roqueta.

*ACAPULCO. Playa de Caleta.*

but, if you place a bet, will give you a genuine sense of participation.

Everyone has his favourite team and however undemonstrative one may be, he will end up completely hoarse after encouraging his team at the Fronton in the Caletilla Garden. The most usual typically Mexican spectacles in Acapulco capital are the charreadas and cock-fighting, and it is easy to get to the places where these sports take place. You can also place bets at the cock-fights, but don't forget it's a crude spectacle in which blood plays a prominent part.

No less colourful, but lacking the cruelty of cockfighting, the charreada offers yet another typically Mexican brand of entertainment. The charreada is the expression of a people who are fond of their domestic animals and have made the horse their inseparable companion, a companion that has first to be trained and broken in using a lassoo, and in doing this the horseman shows his bravery. Although this daring and bravery still exists in the Mexican rodeo, it has been softened slightly by the presence of a show that emphasizes the spectacular and colourful nature of the festivity.

Night life is especially busy in Acapulco, full of unending light and rhythm with pop and rock music and also dreamy romantic nights of languid melodies and the charm of the Mariachis.

You can chose the type of night you would like to spend in Acapulco, — there are all kinds. Nights to be spent on the sea in the moodlight, frenzied nights at dances and entertainment by local or

ACAPULCO. Beaches
Caleta and Caletilla.

ACAPULCO.

ACAPULCO. *Playa de Caleta.*

*ACAPULCO. Yacht Club.*

foreign folklore groups. But before starting out to enjoy a night in Acapulco, don't forget that a night out begins in any of the select restaurants here where you will find the most sophisticated of dishes and also the typical local ones consisting of a strong picant type of cooking that is so different from the cuisine of the rest of the world.

In their gastronomic repertory is the mole, the omlette, quesadillas and so many other exciting things to enjoy, — not once but time and again, for Mexican cooking surprises one, like their beer, which is tasted once and then when the palate is no longer surprised, it surrenders, enamoured of the strong exciting tastes of Mexican food, among which the most unforgettable are the following dishes. El Mole, — a sauce which, according to legend was invented by a nun from Puebla who was preparing a meal for a biship visiting the convent. The legend goes on to tell that the nun dropped some cocoa into the chilli sauce she was making and, having no time to make any more, she mixed the cocoa in with the chilli and served it to the bishop. Apparently the cleric enjoyed the mixture of sweet cocoa with strong chilli, because today el

*ACAPULCO.*

*ACAPULCO*. Pez Vela.

ACAPULCO. Yacht
excursion around the Bay.

*ACAPULCO.*

ACAPULCO. *Handicrafts and artisans.*

*ACAPULCO. San Diego Fort.*

*ACAPULCO. San Diego Fort.*

mole is Mexico's most popular sauce.
The tortilla (omlette) is served as bread and is used to mop up the chilli sauce, it is a pancake of maize which is also used to prepare tacos, enchilados and quesillas.
The taco is a sort of Mexican sandwich with a filling of meat, chicken or cheese. La enchilada is a filling of meat, chicken or cheese cooked in a chilli sauce with onion.
La quesadilla is a sort of cheese filling with the omlette filled with meat, fried beans or cheese.
Among the most popular specialities of Mexican food are, — roast meat à la tampiqueña (beef steaks eaten with bean puré, guacamole (salad made of alligator pear) and bits of omlette served with a chilli sauce), el guajalote con mole poblano (a truly sumptuous dish whose preparation lasts no less than three days and is composed of turkey, different types of peppers, garlic, spices, raisins, and among other ingredients the ever present cocoa), el huachinango à la veracruzana (fish fillets in sauce), stuffed chillis (hot peppers stuffed with meat, almonds and cheese with beaten egg added to them before frying).
Among the curiosities of Mexican gastronomy, mention can be made of nopal leaves, a variety of cactus, and salads of nopalitos, also maguey (agave) worms, served fried as an entrée or apéritif, and turtles' eggs.
Furthermore, Mexico is the paradise of tropical fruit, — pineapples, different kinds of bananas, papayas, mangoes, guavas, mameys, sapodilla plums, Indian figs and custard apples.
In Acapulco, together with the typical Mexican

dishes and tropical fruits you will also find the national beverages, — tequila and el mezcal. Whereas maize is the staple food of the Mexican diet, the maguey (a sort of cactus) is the base of their drinks. Thus, pulque is the product of fermented maguey juice and it is sometimes mixed with fruit which gives it a highly original flavour. Pulque, as we have said, is made simply by fermenting maguey juice, but tequila and mexcal are obtained after distilling it. As they contain a large quantity of alcohol, tequila and mexcal are taken in small sips with a little salt held in the hand. And in Acapulco they drink mezcal Oaxaca style with salt mixed with the explosive powder obtained from maguey worms.

But not only these Mexican liqueurs can be drunk in Acapulco, there is also rum and other refreshing drinks such as tamarind water, chia, jamaica water and coconut water to which a little gin can of course be added.

Throughout the three hundred and sixty five days of the year, the Mexican observes at least a hundred and twenty feast days. Everything is a good reason for the Mexican to sing, dance and laugh ... Mexico is one long party. And not only in Acapulco, but also in other places nearby, where due their rural

*ACAPULCO. The Bay with Icacos in the foreground.*

character the festivities have preserved their pure exotic flavour more completely. Thus to all the cosmopolitan pleasures of Acapulco we can add the no less exciting ones of the nearby towns which are within easy reach of Acapulco for an interesting excursion. In these neighbouring places as in the whole of Mexico, there are three fundamental ingredients for the success of a party: first and foremost, gunpowder, then music and dancing. The Mariachis (a band of guitar players and singers often dressed in charro style) take the well known romantic melodies of crimes or political events around the villages, and there is no baptism, Saints'

day, wedding or party of any sort without Mariachis. It is they who, in the early hours of the morning, sing nostalgic songs of the dawn. For children's parties there is always the piñata, — an earthenware pot filled with sweets, fruit, and small gifts covered with cardboard and multicoloured paper in the shape of an animal or mask which has to be broken by a person who is blindfolded.

Yes, Mexico is certainly one long party and even death is something of a festivity. The Mexican has a very peculiar view of death, probably a more profound and resigned view than those of the other countries of America. It is not surprising therefore

*ACAPULCO. The Pier.*

*ACAPULCO. La Costera (coast road).*

that there is music at burials, for the Mexican laughs and cries when he sings. And he says goodbye to life singing, in the same way in which he has so often said goodbye to some great love in the past. This then is Mexico's way of expressing itself, its passionate and romantic personality, with unusual but most attractive characteristics which you will be able to understand once you feel the magnetic quality of the sun, the air, the moon and the sea at Acapulco.

Your journey around Acapulco is nearing its end, and the city will take its leave of you in an unforgettable way. But before taking the plane or setting off in your car you can still take something with you from Acapulco, something tangible, some piece of local craft work and, if you prefer it, a piece of handwork from any of the states of Mexico,

because the whole of Mexico is in Acapulco. This souvenir can be a silver ornament or piece of jewellery for we must remember that Taxco, the city of silversmiths, is in Guerrero state. It could also be a piece of gold or onyx or natural stone, — blocks of pyrites, quartz, amathyst, turquoise, or opal, not forgetting their pottery and its great variety of shapes and colours. Nor must we forget the amates, those naive drawings with such delightful colours made on the bark of the indian fig tree, although the ladies will prefer sarapes (a sort of shawl made of woven wool) and rebozos, (silk and woollen shawls in bright and in muted colours). And as we are in Acapulco, we must bear in mind that this city is famous for its beach wear. This is an article of clothing which, if it is bought on arrival before beginning your days of sea bathing and parties, will

ACAPULCO.

ACAPULCO.

*Hotel
Acapulco
Continental.*

afterwards serve to remind you of those marvellous days spent in Acapulco whenever you wear it on other occasions.

## CHILPANCINGO

Rather less than 130 kilometres from Acapulco in the direction of Mexico city is Chilpancingo, the capital of Guerrero State.

Chilpancingo is situated in a valley at a height of 1,360 metres above sea level and is a small city with a long history, for it was in Chilpancingo where,

on September 13th 1813 in the middle of the war for Independence, the first Mexican Congress was held, during which Jose Maria Morelos presented his political programme.

Today the tourist can relive the scenes of the Mexican struggle for Independence by visiting the house of the first Revolutionary Congress, a modest colonial style building where this meeting took place, because in this place, in its atmosphere, its corners and also in its stones and furnishings we can read the history of the years which were so decisive in

*ACAPULCO. Parachute ride behind the boat.*

*ACAPULCO.*

ACAPULCO

ACAPULCO.

ACAPULCO. Hotel and bathers.

ACAPULCO

*ACAPULCO. Hotels on the coast road La Costera. Miguel Alemán.*

achieving the independence of the country, that history which was begun in September 1810 by the priest Hidalgo and continued soon after by Jose Maria Morelos, culminating in the proclamation of Independence on February 24th 1821. The corner stone of this history was laid in Chilpancingo in 1813 in the Casa del Primer Congreso Revolucionario, because it was here in this city where Independence was proclaimed by the rebels and where Jose Maria Morelos was made supreme commander of the forces that were to obtain that independence eight years later, and where equality of races and citizenship were decreed. And in Chilpancingo history is continued in the building of the Government Palace, profusely decorated with murals painted by Luis Arenal, Roberto Cuevas del Rio and Gilberto Aceves Navarro, depicting aspects of the Chilpancingo Congress and the Mexican Revolution.

*ACAPULCO. La Concha*
(The Shell).

*Acapulco and the San Diego Fort.*

# COLOTLIPA

Some 50 kilometres from Chilpancingo is Colotlipa, a starting point for a visit to the fantastic Juxtlahuaca caves.

These caves, some of the loveliest human eyes can ever see, are reached by a road some eight kilometres long which is impassable during the rainy season. Everything in the grottos of Juxtlahuaca is more of an adventure than a tourist trip. The caves are still not quite ready for visits and this obliges one to walk for some kilometres underground without any more light than that of a petrol lamp carried by the guide walking in front. But the effort of walking so far is more than compensated by the sight of the innumerable fantastic rooms that nature has sculpted into such strange and fantastic shapes. Juxtlahuaca is a sort of Ali Baba's cave with the incredible wealth produced by millennia of artistic work by nature. The rock has been sculpted by water and man has done the rest, because inside the grotto, more than one kilometre away from the entrance, there is the amazing sight of cave paintings on the walls.

*ACAPULCO. La Concha* (The Shell).

*ACAPULCO. Puerto Marqués.*

*ACAPULCO. Puerto Marqués with the Playa del Revolcadero in the background.*

*Hotel Pierre Marqués and Golf Club.*

These works date from the Olmec period and are contemporaries of those in the Acatlan grottos, but they are different from them in their motifs. In Juxtlahuaca, the main painting is a polychromed one consisting of two people, one of them, of large proportions, is holding a sort of trident and appears to be covering himself with a jaguar skin and is wearing a plumed headdress. The second person, much smaller in size, is seated. A second picture depicts a red serpent and near this second figure there is a third that can be identified as a jaguar. No one doubts that the vast caves at Juatlahuaca guard many other beautiful things in their ornate entrails, both beauties of nature and those forged by the hand of man. For this reason a visit to this place is not only a tourist trip but a whole adventure of discovery, — something truly exciting in this almost completely domesticated world of ours.

## TIXTLA

A few kilometres away from Colotlipa and on the way to the nearby grottos of Acatlan is the city of Tixla, birthplace of Vicente Guerrero, one of the heroes of the War of Independence who gave his name to the state.
Vicente Guerrero was born in 1782 and was one of

*ACAPULCO. Night view.*

*ACAPULCO. The Bay at night.*

*ACAPULCO. Night view.*

Mexico's outstanding figures in the struggle for Independence.

The son of peasants and the descendent of slaves, in his youth he was a muleteer. At the age of 28 he joined the army of Independence, fighting under Morelos. Guerrero then showed such fighting ability, apart from his ethical values, that on the death of Morelos, he became leader of the rebellion in the south of the country. Once independence had been acquired, Guerrero, a just man, expressed his opposition to the despotic régime of Iturbide. And it was his reputation of being an honourable man that made him the second President of the Mexican Republic. However, intrigues soon began to take place, and after being betrayed and subjected to a summary trial in Oaxaca, Guerrero was shot.

Today Toxla preserves his memory as the President under whose mandate slavery in Mexico was finally

*ACAPULCO. Discothèque.*

abolished. From Tixla, the traveller must not forget to visit the nearby town of Chilapa, famous for its rebozos, and the starting point for visiting the Acatlan caves.

The caves at Acatlan are famous for their paintings, the oldest of which date from the Olmec period. On the same wall of rock where the caves are situated, there is one of these paintings, the most valuable according to some. It is a luxuriously dressed human figure seated on the head of a god-jaguar, a divinity of the rain and fertility. Inside the caves there are also large groups of figures painted in red, apart from other monochrome paintings.

## TLAPA

Near to the Acatlan caves, and also to the city of Zitlala and less than 100 kilometres from Chilpancingo, is Tlapa, a Tlapanec town which is

*ACAPULCO. Centre of Conventions.*

*Folklore Ballet in Centre of Conventions.*

certainly worth a visit and one of the few colonization centres in the present day state of Guerrero.

The Augustinians founded a monastery in Tlapa during the XVI century and it is known that in former times the Aztecs possessed garrisons in the mountainous region occupied by the Tlapanecs. The purpose of these garrisons was to collect the taxes imposed on this curious town by the Aztec sovereigns.

Nowadays, a visit to Tlapa is like immersing oneself in history or in an enriching bath of ancient cultures that have seemingly alien concepts but have preserved rites and customs of undoubted value and astounding colour.

The Tlapanecs live mostly in the municipalities of

*ACAPULCO. Sports. Water-skiing. Golf Club.*

*The Bullfighting Ring of El Puerto.*

Ceviche Acapulqueño.

Cocadas *and* tamarindo, *typical sweets of El Puerto.*
*On the floor: Dissected armadillo and turtle.*

Cuttlefish in broth.

*Tropical fruit.*

ACAPULCO. Six views of
coast and beaches.

ACAPULCO. Hotel
Acapulco Princess.

GUERRERO. *Rocks in front of Playa de los Morros del Potosí.*

Malinaltepec, Tlacoapa and Atlamajalcingo, situated to the south of Tlapa. It is a very mountainous region in the heart of the Sierra Madre del Sur. This today is the last refuge of a people who, without any doubt, long ago occupied a much larger geographical area, a people who were attacked, whom the Aztecs fought and overcame, but who never became subject and for that reason today still evidence some peculiarly original features.
Thus, the Tlapanec communities, although subjected to federal laws, continue to preserve as a local power institution, a council of elders which on occasion is substituted by a leader. And every change in municipal power is marked by a solemn ceremony called the change of rods, in which the rod of justice passes from the person in power to the one substituting him.
The Tlapanec economy is essentially rural, almost

primitive. They live off the land which produces maize, beans, sugar cane and tobacco; there is also a handicraft tradition and their straw hats are famous.
The Tlapanecs live in simple dwellings made from logs, often with a roof of palm leaves. But the most important aspect of the Tlapanecs is not their primitive way of life and their persistent dependence on the land but the consequence of all this, — their ceremonies and rites especially those of a religious kind.
The Tlapanecs are Catholic but this does not hinder their abservance of traditions and rites dating from the prehispanic period. Thus they still worship the goddess Earth, the god of Rain and the gods of the Mountains.
The Tlapanecs, who worship the mountain tops and even the tops of smaller hills, light up their sacred

ACAPULCO. Late afternoon in Puerto Marqués.

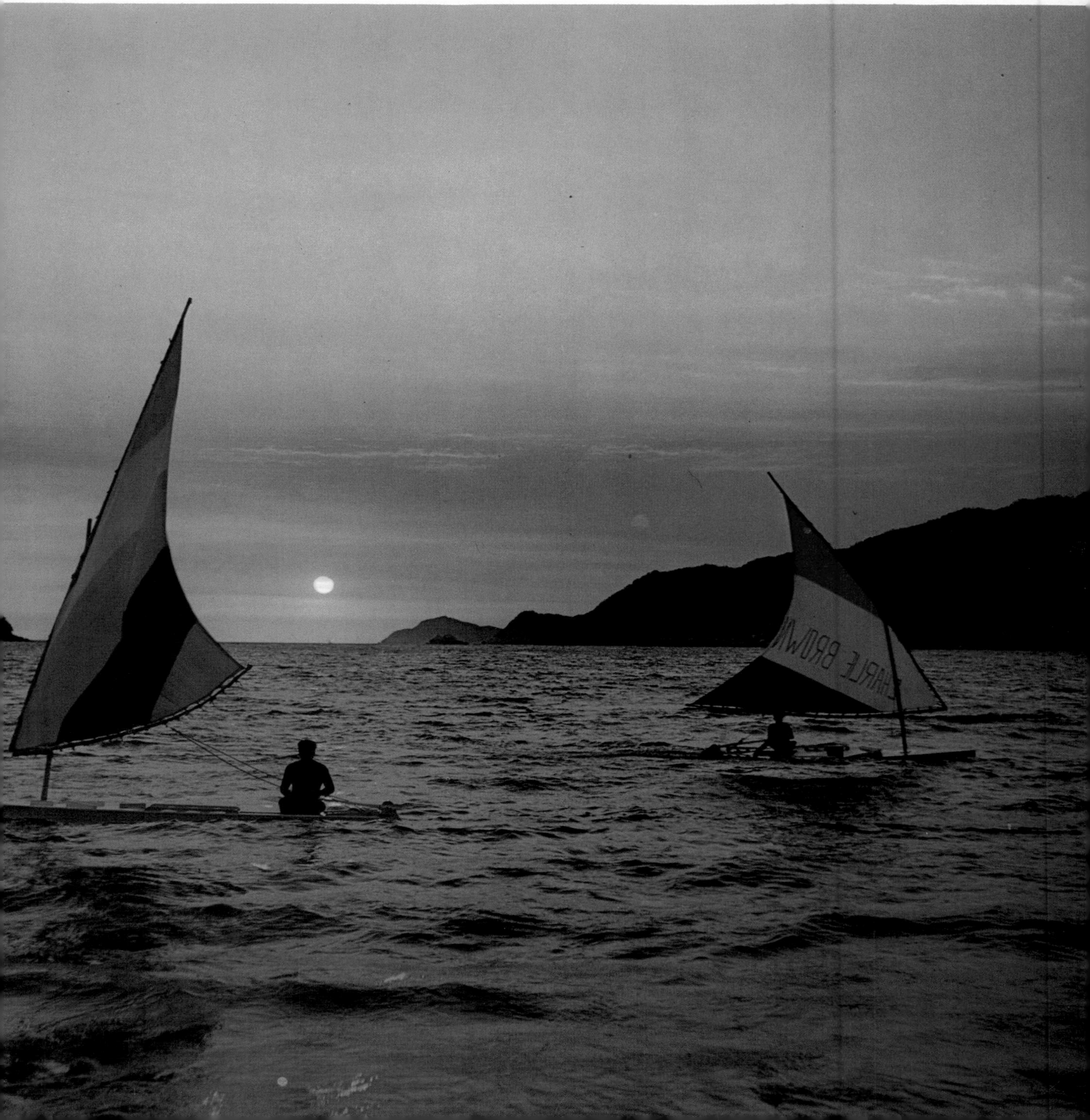

*Woman with typical Guerrero costume.*

*Guerrero dancers.*

grottos with candles and leave offerings of food there, accompanying this act with the ritual beating of drums and the ritual sound of the chirimias. These magic rites of the Tlapanecs are abviously connected with the seasons of the year and are ceremonies especially linked to the need for rain and the desire for good harvests. In a community like that of the Tlapanecs there are few events and happenings that are not associated with magic ceremonies. So even the burial of the dead is accompanied by a ritual banquet, usually shared with any visitor, which includes el mole de guajalote, beans with chilli sauce and tamals, taken with a chocolate type of drink.

But the Tlapanec indians not only worship their tribal gods but also celebrate the Catholic religious festivals including those of the feast day of each one of the patron saints of their towns. And these celebrations take place with processions, music, fireworks, and dances, — among them the most characteristic of these people's repertoire, — the chichipelado.

*Guerrero dancers.*

Needless to say, a visit to Tlapanec villages especially on their feast days or on the days when they celebrate their ritual ceremonies, is a unique experience, an unforgettable enriching sight, for the magic sense of life of the Tlapanecs makes us enter unknown areas of the human mind, — far from the limited view of life of the so-called civilized western world.

## IGUALA

Slightly nearer to the capital, Mexico City, on the way to Taxco is the city of Iguala.

Founded in 1750 Iguala is a historic city that had its most important moment in the so-called Plan of the Three Guarantees proclaimed on February 24th 1821.

With the Plan of the Three Guarantees, also known as the Iguala Plan, Augustin de Iturbide took a decisive step on the road to Independence in Mexico. And the city is conscious of this fact. The visitor can see this in the streets, buildings and monuments at Iguala.

## TAXCO

The present city of Taxco is derived from the ancient Tlaxco (pelota game) located some 12 kilometres away in a place called Taxco el Viejo, near some important silver and tin mines.

In the middle of the XV century Itzcoatl invaded the region of ancient Tlaxco and the city was annexed to the Aztec kingdom during the reign of Moctezuma.

Conquered by the Spaniards in 1522, the Tlaxco region soon showed itself to be an inexhaustible source of mineral wealth as successive prospecting, which initially had been looking only for the tin necessary for the making of bronze artillery pieces, also revealed the presence of large deposits of silver on the slopes of the Cerro de Barmeja. And it was the presence of the camps established by these new silver mines that originated the now important city of Taxco.

In the XVIII century a certain Jose de la Borda whom the French suppose to have been born in Gasconia and the Spanish in Jaca, gave a new dynamism to Taxco, apart from amassing an immense personal fortune, when he began to exploit the San Ignacio mine. The mine proved so rich that Jose de la Borda

ZIHUATANEJO.
*Playa La Madera.*
*Hotel Calpulli.*
*La Ropa and Hotel Sotovento.*

IXTAPA. *Hotel Presidente.*

IXTAPA. *Golf field.*

IXTAPA. *Hotel Arístos.*

*Hotel Caracol at Zihuatanejo.*

could allow himself the luxury of defraying the costs of the building of the church of Santa Trisca, one of the marvels of Mexican churrigueresque art. And this pious gesture on the part of the wealthy Jose de la Borda was accompanied by another of a more secular description, — fountains for the city of Taxco.

After a period of decline in the silver manufacturing industry, Taxco flowered once again when the Canadian William Sprating arrived there; he was a man of great commercial insight who gave impetus to the hand-made jewellery industry in the region. Nowadays, Taxco has almost 2,000 craftsmen working in silver in some 100 workshops. These craftsmen with their refined taste in making jewellery and ornaments use an alloy of silver and copper in which the proportion of metal is from 950 to 980 gms. of silver to between 20 and 50 gms. of copper.

Obviously Taxco is today the silver city par excellence, but it is not a large city although certainly a hospitable one, situated at a height of 1660 metres

*Late evening on the Guerrero coastline.*

*Santa Prisca church in Taxco.*

and with streets cut out of the rock and houses with portals and many baroque churches that give it an air of a town is Castile.

Looking at Taxco from afar is to have the impression of a scene from the colonial period. On the slopes of Mount Atachi, a bastion of the Cerro de Bermeja, the low built houses with red tiles appear to want to climb up into the sky. They seem to advance in a procession, pressed tightly together, hesitating in their climb, making mazes of doubt along with the cart tracks and the little streets of the ancient city, with the shouts of children in the sun and the peal of bells.

The church of Santa Prisca, the most imposing monument in the city, stands in the Zocalo, or Plaza de la Borda, — a pleasant square shaded by indian laurels and surrounded by historic buildings among them the one built in the first half of the XVIII century by the plutocrat Jose de la Borda.

As for the majestic church of Santa Prisca, it was built in less than ten years, between 1748 and 1758. And all the expenses incurred in its construction were paid by Jose de la Borda, the man who filled his coffers with the proceeds of the mine at San Ignacio.

The church of Santa Prisca is a genuine product of

*TAXCO. Cross in Santa Prisca.*

*TAXCO. Sacristy of the Santa Prisca church; XVIII century paintings by Miguel Cabrera.*

*TAXCO.*
*High-altar*
*of the Santa*
*Prisca church.*

the imagination of a tropical country. Its facade, laden to the utmost with baroque decoration, prolongs its tropical exuberance into every corner of every wall in this unique church.
The main door of Santa Prisca opens between two pillars with corinthian columns. And not only this door, but the whole of the facade is an enormous construction filled with sculptures, among them a bas relief representing the Baptism of Christ. On the

remaining parts are an enormous tiara, cherubim and designs of vegetation which give the impression of wanting to climb up all the stones in the church walls.
In contrast, the two towers on either side of the facade are amazingly sober for approximately half of their length. But beyond this point the florid churrigueresque imagination of the builders overflowed once more with more decorative

*TAXCO.*

*TAXCO. Spratling Museum.*

elements, although the ornamental work is done with such delicacy that the sculptures seem to have been carved out of jade.

And this fantasmagorical but valuable churrigueresque style is carried on into the interior of the church of Santa Prisca where magnificent pictures decorated with gold plates seem like jewels set in the sculpted stone and are profusely worked in harmony with the whole architectural concept. It is an apotheosis in stone and paint of Saints, prelates, rosy angels, fruit and flowers. The large tympanum of Santa Prisca, that enormous architectural half moon situated above the gate of the Capilla del Padre Jesús or the Capilla de los Indios, is decorated with a valuable painting by Miguel Cabrera depicting the martyrdom of Santa Prisca decapitated in the Coliseum in Rome about the year 270.

*MEZCALA. Typical archaeological figures from the State of Guerrero.*

*TAXCO. Spratling Museum — Silver and Mexican-Olmec archaeological objects.*

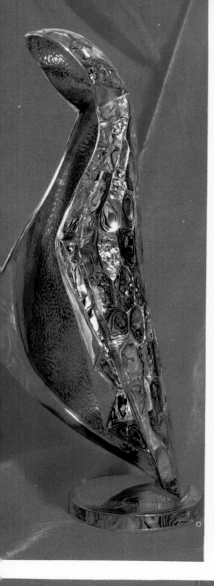

TAXCO.

*TAXCO.* Mural painting by O'Gorman, representing The Mission *in the Hotel Posada.*

*TAXCO.* Casa Verdugo Aragonés.

TAXCO.

TAXCO. *The Humboldt House.*

Miguel Cabrera, the great early XVIII century painter
is also present in other works to be found in the
sacristy and another of his works is a medallion
depicting the suffering of souls in Purgatory.
After the visit to Santa Prisca we are once more in
el Zocalo in the tropical sunlight shaded by trees
and cornices, and we will now go for a short walk
through the streets of Taxco.
If you go down the calle del Arco, to one side of
Santa Prisca, you will soon reach the market. Go
there on Saturdays and Sundays when it is
particularly busy, — it is quite an adventure, an
adventure from which you can emerge with a find
in the shape of a genuine piece of treasure. To go
shopping in Taxco is to discover many extremely
pleasant things.
In the Guerrero gardens, after having walked along
the calle Real de San Nicolás, we can admire the
church of la Santisima, rebuilt in baroque style in
1713.
In the nearby plaza de San Juan is the Town Hall
building, — a vast XVIII century construction and the
former seat of the Royal Mining Society of Taxco.
It is the so-called Casa Grande or Casa Real where
Jose Maria Morelos stayed in 1811.
You must not forget to go to the nearby calle de
Ojeda. There, from the church of el Señor de Ojeda,
built in 1822 on the top of a hill, you can enjoy a
panoramic view of the whole of the city of Taxco.

Back again in el Zocalo, you must not miss the calle Real de San Agustin, possibly the only street without a slope in the entire city. But you don't have to go there simply because it's the only level road, which in Taxco is something really unusual, but because it is the street in which there are many souvenir shops and jewellers. This is where you can find all the silverware from the workshops at Taxco. In the plaza de los Gallos, close to the calle Real de San Agustin, there is the surprising sight of a part of the Sevillian district of Santa Cruz. The same little whitewashed houses, shining in the sun with lanterns and flower pots and a fountain. It is the blue, scented, Moorish Andalusia itself.

From the nearby church of the Virgin of Guadalupe built in 1877 on the site of a small sanctuary dating from the first half of the XVIII century, you can also see, as you did from the church of el Señor de Ojeda, the whole of the city in a panoramic view which allows you to take an impressive photograph including the whole of the church of Santa Prisca. The Casa de Villanueva or Casa Humboldt, close by the calle Juan Ruiz de Alarcon has a majestic mudejar facade. This valuable building erected by Juan de Villanueva in the XVIII century was the residence of baron von Humboldt, although curiously he only actually stayed there for one night. There are other historical and artistic buildings

*TAXCO. A nice area in the city.*

in Taxco like the chapel of el Señor de Chavarrieta, with its fine XVII century crucifix; the Municipal Palace with its watch tower; and the former convent of San Bernardino founded towards the end of the XVI century by the Franciscans.

And on the road leading to Cuernavaca are the ruins of a silver furnace where it is possible to discover almost the complete process of the transformation of the mineral into metal. And not far away, on the road to Iguala is the sanctuary of la Cruz de la Mision, a small church built in the year 1817 on the same site that was occupied by a much older chapel. Inside the chapel are some naif paintings of outstanding beauty, ex votos and a crucifix which,

according to tradition possesses miraculous powers. Opposite this sanctuary on the stone facade of an old mission is a plaque reminding us that the dramatist Juan Ruiz de Alarcon was born in Taxco at the end of the XVI century.

But Taxco is not just a city filled with monuments even though it has been officially declared a national monument; in Taxco the visitor can also enjoy all the picturesque quality of Mexican popular festivities with their colourful amateur bull fights and the intermingling of the local dances, but even so, the great entertainment in Taxco is still that very popular sport known as shopping. Because in Taxco shopping is an endless pleasure. The local craft

*TAXCO. The little Plaza de San Juan.*

Exterior of a handicraft shop.

Silver from Taxco.

Guerrero handicraft.

*Guerrero paintings and so-called* laca. *The paintings are made on* amate *paper in the village of Ameyaltepec.*

work in silver fills the shops and offers the widest variety of goods. Taxco not only has the fantastic baroque church of Santa Prisca but the baroque imagination of its fine metal craftsmen, and so, jewels, vases and all kinds of ornaments and objets d'art are of the most varied shapes and styles. The jewels that you can and must buy in Taxco can be in the purest and most ancient of local styles, but they can also be in contemporary designs like the styles of jewels created by Dali.

Don't forget then, that the art of silverware awaits you in Taxco. So when you get there start that enjoyable sport of shopping in Taxco and bear in mind that among the most creditable of the silver-smiths' workshops are those belonging to the Castillo brothers, Salvador Teran, and Antonio Pineda, not forgetting the Casa Mujia, which has put the designs created by William Sprating on the market once more. And although we have

mentioned a few names, all the silverware in Taxco is of great beauty and highly valued, because the whole city is one great workshop and its inhabitants, every one of them, are the heirs of a unique and ancient craft tradition.

## CACAHUAMILPA

Leaving Taxco you can visit the caves at Cacahuamilpa and bathe in the freezing waters of an underground lake.

Discovered in 1835 these caves are at a height of 1,105 metres in the so-called Cerro de la Corona. Created by two rivers and stretching for almost 100 kms., up to now only 8 kms. of the caves have been explored. It is therefore, possibly one of the largest ever known, and of exceptional beauty, with chambers having an average height of 40 metres. The stretch of caves explored up to the present time is well illuminated and in good condition, 15 chambers can be visited by the public, all of them of an almost unparalleled beauty. Nature has created scenes of the most surprising fantasy, sculpting stalactites and stalagmites, creating shapes and forms of the most evocative and bewitching kinds. Sometimes the sculpture is in miniature, the result of the constant dripping of calcareous water onto the vast overwhelming mass of kilometres and kilometres of caves with vaults that become lost in a telluric sky.

As in the Juxtlahuaca caves, you can, if you are fond of speleology, try to explore them. A completely virgin world, untouched by man lies before you. There are hundreds of natural cathedrals to be explored, hundreds of still hidden marvels in the bowels of the earth that can be brought to light; it is an adventure in search of beauty, the most gransiose beauty imaginable created by God, and you can be one of the first to see this divine work of art.

*IGUALA. Monument of Independence.*

*IGUALA.*

*Grottos of Cacahuamilpa. These three «rooms» are only a part of the 15 which at present can be easily visited and are perfectly illuminated. The medium height, i.e. from bottom to top, is 40 metres.*

*Grottos of Cacahuamilpa.*

But if you decide not to risk your life by journeying into the virgin depths of the earth, don't let that worry you as it is possible to see eight kilometres of the caves extremely comfortably. And even though others have seen them before you, it still gives a thrill of discovery and is an impressive sight indeed.

## ZIHUATANEJO

Acapulco is the tourist capital of Guerrero State's coastline, but this does not mean that there can't be any beaches to rival those of Acapulco on the same stretch of coastline. In fact the whole coastline of this state is a succession of narrow plains of fine sand between lagoons. They are beaches with the charm of having summer weather guaranteed.

Although today they do not possess the hotel facilities of Acapulco, many of these beaches will one day rival Acapulco itself, and some of them, like Zihuatanejo are already on the way to doing so. Zihuatanejo is a small fishing port established some 100 years ago. Located on a sheltered bay, its only activity until recently was the export and purchase of bananas, but like Acapulco, the bay has many beaches with fine sand separated by tree-covered hills or crags. For this reason it has become a highly appreciated summer resort, especially for those who are looking for a peaceful place to stay. However, Zihuatanejo is still in the process of becoming a summer resort and is gradually growing in importance. Hotels are emerging one after another and the architecture in the area is planned and in tune with the environment.

*Grottos of Juxtlahuaca. Olmec cave paintings.*

*Organ.*

The Ixtapa area is also involved in the ambitious projects for this region.

## IXTAPA

Ten kilometres away from Zihuatanejo along the route of the playa Azul stands Ixtapa, an enormous project which has begun to be a reality as its first hotels have now been inaugurated.

The project consists of creating a practically new city on a small piece of flat land and on some hills along a stretch of coastline 20 kilometres long, having a main beach 6 kilometres long and many coves and inlets like those of El Palmar, Don Juan, Quieta, Don Rodrigo, Las Cuatas and Hermosa. All these coves and beaches are close to a lagoon that has preserved its original flora and fauna. Ixtapa has already been put on the drawing beard and is beginning to be a tangible reality with luxurious hotels, eighteen hole golf courses, a sailing club and a harbour for yachts... A complete city has been projected which it is thought will one day rival Acapulco itself. Will this be an impossible challenge? Mexico has produced an Acapulco; why then can't it produce another and repeat the miracle of one of its most prodigious achievements?

*Lagoon of Chilpancingo.*

# CIUDAD ALTAMIRANO

This is a small city that stands in the valley of the river Balsas and has the most luxuriant tropical vegetation.

The natural beauty of Ciudad Altamirano is complemented by the proximity of Coyuca de Catalan which, at the beginning of the XV century was the seat of the small Tarascan principality governed by Hiripan who was succeeded by his son Ticatame, who in his turn became a fief of the king Tzintzuntzan.

Also, close to Arcelia, on the way to Iguala from Ciudad Altamirano you are within easy reach of the archaeological area of Los Monos. This is an area of pyramidical constructions built on platforms and is a place with some fascinating sculptures and sites used for the pelota game.

The archaeological area of Los Monos, (the name was given to it by the local population) probably dates from the VII and VIII centuries A.D. It is a fine example of ancient Mexico, of the Mexico which, in Guerrero state, offers the visitor the widest view of its history, the exotic beauty of its landscapes, the most curious of local customs, in addition to the bewitching magic of Acapulco.

*Guerrero coastline during full moon.*

# ESTADO DE GUERRERO

MICHOACAN

ESTADO DE MEXICO

MEXICO D.F.

PUEBLA

MORELOS

ALTAMIRANO

TELOLOAPAN

IGUALA

HUITZUCO

TLAPEHUALA

ZUMPANGO

CHILAPA

ESTADO

TIXLA

Bahia Petalcalco

DE

CHILPANCINGO

Bahia Potosi

ZIHUATANEJO

PETATLAN

GUERRERO

OAXACA

TECPAN

TENEXPA

ATOYAC

Laguna Nuxco

COYUCA DE BENITEZ

ACAPULCO

Laguna Mitla

OCEANO

L. de Coyuca

Laguna de Tres Palos

SAN MARCO

PACIFICO

L. de Tecomate

CRUZ GRANDE

COPATA

L. de Chanlongo

OMETEPEC

GUAJINICUILAPA

Punta Maldonado

# ACAPULCO

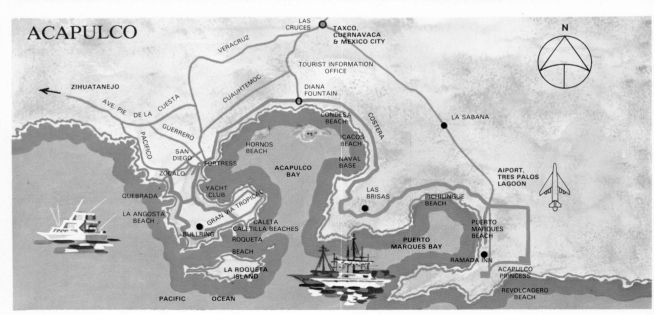

LAS CRUCES

TAXCO, CUERNAVACA & MEXICO CITY

N

VERACRUZ

TOURIST INFORMATION OFFICE

ZIHUATANEJO

DIANA FOUNTAIN

CUAUHTEMOC

AVE. PIE DE LA CUESTA

CONDESA BEACH

COSTERA

LA SABANA

GUERRERO

ICACOS BEACH

PACIFICO

HORNOS BEACH

SAN DIEGO

ACAPULCO BAY

NAVAL BASE

AIPORT, TRES PALOS LAGOON

FORTRESS

ZOCALO

YACHT CLUB

LAS BRISAS

QUEBRADA

GRAN VIA TROPICAL

PICHILINGUE BEACH

LA ANGOSTA BEACH

PUERTO MARQUES BEACH

CALETA CALETILLA BEACHES

BULLRING

ROQUETA BEACH

PUERTO MARQUES BAY

RAMADA INN

ACAPULCO PRINCESS

LA ROQUETA ISLAND

REVOLCADERO BEACH

PACIFIC OCEAN

# INDEX

Printed in Spain   GEOCOLOR®
M.R.-TM